GREAT MASTERPIECES BY

FREDERIC
Remington

GREAT MASTERPIECES BY

FREDERIC
Remington

BY LOUIS CHAPIN

AN **Artabras** BOOK

CROWN PUBLISHERS, INC. • NEW YORK, N.Y.

On the front cover:
Indian Warfare

On the title page:
A Dash for the Timber

On the back cover:
Coming Through the Rye

Commentaries on page 104

Library of Congress Catalog Card Number: 79-67178

ISBN: 0-517-30507-0

CONTENTS

Indian Warfare . . . . FRONT COVER
Commentary 104

A Dash for the Timber . . . . TITLE PAGE
Commentary 104

An Indian Trapper 10–11

Episode of a Buffalo Hunt 12–13

Hungry Moon 14–15

A Cavalryman's Breakfast on the Plains 16–17

The Scout: Friends or Enemies? 18–19

The Old Stage Coach of the Plains 20–21

A Snowbound Christmas on the
Overland Coach 22–23

Ridden Down 24–25

Victory Dance 26–27

Through the Smoke Sprang the
Daring Young Soldier 28–29

Battle of Warbonnet Creek 30–31

A Reconnaissance 32–33

Pony Tracks in the Buffalo Trails 34–35

The Smoke Signal 36–37

The Stampede 38–39

Coming and Going of the Pony Express 40–41

Cavalryman of the Line, Mexico, 1889 42–43

Drum Corps, Mexican Army, 1889 44–45

With the Eye of the Mind 46–47

His First Lesson 48–49

The Discovery 50–51

The Night Rider 52–53

Missing 54–55

The Cowboy 56–57

The Fall of the Cowboy 58–59

The Long-Horn Cattle Sign 60–61

The Bell Mare 62–63

The Cavalry Charge 64–65

The Grass Fire 66–67

The Outlier 68–69

The Bronco Buster 70–71

The Wounded Bunkie 72–73

The Cheyenne 74–75

The Outlaw 76–77

The Mountain Man 78–79

The Old Dragoons of 1850 80–81

The Scalp 82–83

The Horse Thief 84–85

Paleolithic Man 86–87

The Buffalo Horse 88–89

The Stampede 90–91

Trooper of the Plains 92–93

The Wicked Pony 94–95

The Savage 96–97

The Sergeant 98–99

The Rattlesnake 100–101

The Norther 102–103

Coming Through the Rye . . . . BACK COVER
Commentary 104

INTRODUCTION

by LOUIS CHAPIN

"ART," WROTE FREDERIC REMINGTON in 1905, "is a she-devil of a mistress, and if at times in earlier days she would not even stoop to my way of thinking, I have persevered and will so continue."

He had just been describing one particular "earlier day" around a Montana campfire in 1881, when an old-timer who had also come out there from New York and had since spent his life following the frontier, convinced him that "there is no more West." At which point Remington decided to "try to record some facts around me."

So doing, he not only aimed himself towards a lucrative career, but helped to inaugurate the world-wide bonanza called the Old West, or the Wild West, of which there would always seem to be more. This would have interested Remington Senior, a man of somewhat venturesome but practical affairs, who was chagrined when in 1879 his son chose the art school at Yale instead of a business course. Young Frederic was even more chagrined when he got there and found at the art school a classic approach to art principles and to drawing. That was when he first noticed the she-devil refusing to stoop.

Frederic felt she should be down where he was, making pictures. He'd been doing so through most of his childhood in upstate New York, where he had been born in Canton in 1861. By the time his family moved to Ogdensburg eleven years later, he'd already made pictures of actual firehorses and of imaginary frontier battle scenes, and in 1875 his first painting was a glowering *Captive Gaul,* done on a window shade.

In college Remington escaped the haughty she-devil for a while on the historic varsity football team of 1879, and as a heavyweight boxer—for both of which sports he was already heftily qualified. Then in 1880 his father died, Yale was abandoned, and after a year or so of clerical jobs Frederic followed his imagination west, as far as Arizona and Indian Territory. And on that trip he met the man who was all out of frontiers.

"There is no more West." Remington's lifelong answer to that man—who like other characters of his could have been real or made-up—was both agreement and denial. It was to say, in effect, "Alright, the West is dead. Long live the West." Long live whose West? His, of course. He couldn't do anything about the old man's lost West. He couldn't take his eye and his sketch pad back into time past, and there's little to indicate he wanted to—even later on, after his West seemed to be contaminated by the East. Though many of his paintings and drawings over the years would be staging bygone Western scenes—and as convincingly as possible—his "facts" would be "the facts around" him as he saw them then.

Those would have to do with a place roomy enough to cherish a young country's adolescence, to allow all-boy behavior further away from the adult constraints of Europe—a place, in a way, to escape art. As a frontier place it gave breathing space to the lifelong, tough youthfulness in Remington, the outdoorsman and incipient soldier, as it did for his collaborator and friend Theodore Roosevelt, and many others.

Remington's facts, then, were not so much scenic, or even historic, as they were human. The facts, above all, were "men with the bark on," to use his own blithely chauvinistic phrase—*and* their horses. Cowboys, prospectors, soldiers, Indians—he gave them such energetic reality that some of them who aren't otherwise occupied seem to be mainly concerned with catching our attention.

And they deserve it. Remington's gift was a huge one, a boyish one, a strongly journalistic and illustrative one, coupled easily with his secondary gift for words. It became harder for him to join it with his evolving aspirations as an artist, coaxed as he was by that she-devil. The joining never seemed complete.

Meanwhile, finding facts as any kind of reporter meant also finding publishers for the facts, and it took four or five years to get into full production and distribution. During this time Remington married his friend Eva Caten, failed as a Kansas rancher and investor, sold a scattering of pictures, foraged around Mexico on the trail of Geronimo, and tried a little more art study in New York. The angular, "bark-on" vitality of his pictures needed to find acceptance by an editorial art-consciousness which was then marked by gentility, serenity, allegorical moralizing, and a few other refinements that hadn't brushed off on Remington at Yale or anywhere else.

The door to success, when it opened wide one day in 1886,

happened to be the door to the offices of *Outing Magazine,* whose weary editor turned out with sudden jubilation to be Poultney Bigelow, a cohort from those Yale days: as editor of the *Courant* he had run Remington's cartoons. But even before he recognized his old friend, Bigelow had recognized the Western gold in his pictures. He bought the entire portfolio, ordered more, and soon the editors of *Harper's Weekly, Scribner's,* and other established periodicals, who had previously bought a drawing or two, stepped up their interest.

"These [pictures showed] the men of the real rodeo," Bigelow later wrote, "parched in alkali dust, blinking out from barely opened eyelids under the furious rays of an Arizona sun." The old man's West might be gone; but Remington's cowboys and soldiers were *there*. Gentility, even in the East, had to give them room.

Recognition as a visual reporter was naturally welcome. But already it wasn't enough. Beyond the new tours and assignments (including a disappointing one to Russia, Europe, and Africa in 1892 and a grueling one to Cuba with the Rough Riders in 1898), and beyond the illustrating of such authors as Owen Wister, Longfellow, Roosevelt, and of course Remington himself, there began to be the heady stuff of well-received gallery showings. And not only at home: his work won a Silver Medal at the 1889 Paris Exposition. Then in 1891 came an associate membership in the National Academy.

For all that, it was the good business of the magazine illustrations—the Old West he was renewing—that was now meaning prosperity for the Remingtons. In 1890 they moved out from New York to a house in New Rochelle with room for a library-studio, and for his constantly growing collection of Western props and clothing. Enjoying its views over the water and the Westchester countryside, he gave it an Algonquin Indian name: Endion, "a place where I live." By 1906, however, he felt crowded even there. (Remington, who had been described by a young army friend years before as "a big, good-natured, overgrown boy [whose] gait was an easy waddle," was something of a crowd all by himself.) A still bigger house and studio (Remington looked leisurely, but he worked hard) were built in 1908 on thirteen acres in Ridgefield, Connecticut. It was just a year later—the day after Christmas, 1909—that Remington died after an operation for appendicitis.

But fifteen years before that his negotiations with the she-devil had brought about a whole new range. One of Remington's New Rochelle neighbors was Frederic W. Ruckstull, a successful sculptor. During the early summer of 1895 Ruckstull was at work on a monumental commission. Remington found himself watching with interest, and by late that fall, with some prodding from Ruckstull, he had given shape to his own first sculpture. He took easily and zestfully to modeling in clay, and kept doing so—along with his painting—from this first *Bronc Buster* to the *Stampede* of his last months in 1909. His later casting into bronze was done by the venerable lost wax method, under Riccardo Bertelli's skilled guidance at the Roman Bronze Works on Long Island.

Remington's success in every medium rested on his sure dramatic instincts and on his sense of the *scene*—the whole lively interest of an event that depended neither on well-known people nor on an allegorical message for its effect, but simply on an emphatic interaction or (in the case of a single figure) a well-bitten characterization. This gift, which showed vividly in the painting and impressively in the sculpture, was and is important to Remington's credentials as an artist. So also is the strong color emphasis that brought compelling mood into the night scenes of his last decade. During this time he was on good terms with some of the new American impressionists; Childe Hassam was a particular friend. Their example encouraged in him an impressionistic corrosion of daytime and sunset colors by light. The critics, on the whole, approved of his results, though occasionally professing to miss the old clarity.

Pleased as he was to be working (though hardly making his ample living) as an artist, Remington seemed to feel at times that he hadn't yet chosen a single, definable career. In that 1905 comment he implied that the she-devil of art had at last decided to "stoop" to his way of thinking, but that perseverance was still needed. It was as though the artist and the illustrator in him had never really taken the full measure of each other, didn't quite trust each other.

Might it not be possible, after three quarters of a century, to bring these two roles together as one achievement, to enjoy the cross-pollination between realistic reportage and creative vision? With all Remington's perseverance this was difficult for him, and critics today still seem to find the job bothersome. In the first place, it's a nuisance when an artist spills from one classification to another. We prefer people whom we can sort out and label: painter, sculptor, impressionist, hard-edge realist, or whatever. Please, not all four in one man! Run him through the sorter again, and he probably comes out, like Daumier, a journalist who did some Sunday painting. Masterpieces? Impossible.

And then there are those many-faceted Remingtonian chauvinisms, from all-boy to all-American. Does that last, we ask pointedly, take in the American Indian? Sure, Remington went to Wounded Knee and was close to the massacre, but did he even know the right questions, let alone the answers?

It may be useful to remind ourselves that Remington was much nearer the hostilities than we are, and that the army he so admired did not, after all, start the war. He probably would have agreed with General George Crook, an early veteran of frontier service, who when asked what he found hardest in the Indian wars, said this: "The hardest thing is to fight against those whom you know are right."

The present book is one more sampling of art by this restless and protean figure. As such, it can offer a varied overview.

And if we are not satisfied that any one work is either commanding enough or self-enlightened enough to be a masterpiece, perhaps the juxtaposition of two will help. There is a pair here, for instance, dealing with a sequence of events at the 1879 Battle of Warbonnet Creek, another miserable anticlimax of nineteenth-century Indian policy. Remington painted the two scenes for *Harper's Weekly* about seven years after Wounded Knee. Since they have been separated since his lifetime in different collections, their reunion here may be to the benefit of each.

No, the artist doesn't show American soldiers to be monsters, as these Indians are finally cornered and exterminated. Why should he? The job was a tough one, and demanded bravery. Yet neither does he suggest, even in the title, that these men are saviors of their country. Though he accepts the simplistic term "bushwhacking" for this kind of operation, he brings to its dirty work a reasonable objectivity. More than that, he brings an artist's consummate skill and—it seems possible—a beginning of incredulity.

A good many of his peers were no doubt still mouthing the old "only-good-Indian-a-dead-Indian" maxim. Not so this "chauvinist." The soldiers he paints here are of course dogged and tired, the ones who are still standing. But there's a stunned look to them as well. And there's something in their eyes—and therefore in the artist's mind—asking "What are we doing?" and "What have we done?"

It may turn out, in the longer view, that Frederic Remington was an educable journalist who was also—and sometimes in the same inseparable act—a master artist.

Frederic Sackrider Remington (1861–1909)

An Indian Trapper

(1889) *Oil on canvas* · *49⅛ × 34¼"* · *Amon Carter Museum, Fort Worth, Texas*

THOUGH NOT ONE OF Remington's story-telling scenes, this meeting with an Indian trapper is one of the most widely reproduced. In the first place, it *is* a meeting: the man isn't just passing by, or holding a pose for the artist. He has stopped and turned in his awkward saddle with the short stirrups and is returning the artist's look of interest. He can't wait long, obviously, because he must keep up with his cohorts along the trail. And those far-ranging peaks give us a sense of distances to go before the day is done. The Western majesty is waiting, and we are pulled toward it through the intent of this impatient man, clad in the English blanket coat of the Hudson's Bay Company, and painted with sharp, emphatic reality.

We are pulled also by the zig-zag strategy of composition. The scrawny horse (especially so in its neck and forequarters) points toward the left, the two other trappers moving away at right angles. These directions are repeated in the mountain ridges beyond, and their meeting point is just above the trapper's fur cap. Our eye moves easily, then, through the inverted Y of his body and off into the mountainous distances.

Though many trappers were whites, for the Indian (this one probably Cree or Blackfoot) trapping provided a uniquely profitable alternative to watching his country being taken over. Through it he could share a little in the fur-trading bonanza of the northern regions.

Episode of a Buffalo Hunt

(1908) *Oil on canvas · 28½ × 26½" · Gilcrease Institute, Tulsa, Oklahoma*

CHARLES M. RUSSELL, more than any other painter, explored the variegated drama of the buffalo hunt, which for the Indian was a vital source of food, clothing, housing, and much else. But Remington brought off a unique three-way encounter in this late, rather impressionistically styled painting. He gave it sculptural treatment as well, under the title of *The Buffalo Horse,* and you may wish to compare the two works.

The buffalo was not a particularly bright or nimble animal. An experienced Indian with an equally experienced horse could usually work in close, shoot an arrow through the hide just behind the shoulder, and break away quickly to avoid any swerving by the enraged beast.

But this swerve must have been a surprising one. The buffalo's ton or so of propulsive weight has in an instant stopped and lifted the horse, and the rider's momentum has carried him somersaulting over the horse's head.

The force and the counterforce in the collision, however locked together compositionally, are carefully distinguished. The buffalo, through its loose, light-soaked color and texture, is a force in harmony with the natural growth in the background; the ruddier coloring and firmer drawing of the hunter and his horse, on the other hand, meet this brute force with a swiftness of line and form. Though at this moment it is disastrously airborne, in the longer term it represents at least an equal match.

Hungry Moon

(1900) *Oil on canvas* · *19½ × 25½"* · *Gilcrease Institute, Tulsa, Oklahoma*

THE GRADUAL CHANGE IN emphasis from Remington the journalist/illustrator to Remington the artist can be seen in a growing fascination with light and color—and as often as not with moonlight, with its way of simplifying and mystifying the effects of color. Charles Rollo Peters had become famous for his "moonlights," and Remington the artist was spurred by seeing an exhibit of Peters's work. "The mystery of these efforts and their largeness were keyed to the mute though not inglorious poet in him," wrote Remington's playwright friend Augustus Thomas.

Often the moonlight brings a note of fantasy to the hard reality of the actual scene: in this case, the plundering of a fallen buffalo for meat. The Indian had ways of using practically every part of this animal, from its hide for tents, ropes, and clothing to the dung for fuel. But for this handful—family, perhaps—of night riders, food is the most urgent need.

Remington generally spreads either a deep blue or (as here) a green over his nighttime scenes, with perhaps a few pungent touches of orange firelight or window light for contrast. In this lonely scene there is no such warmth; the light is reflected all round the huddle of figures, who seem hardly touched by it, and far from any light of comfort. It's almost as though they were *on* the moon.

A Cavalryman's Breakfast on the Plains

(c. 1890) *Oil on canvas · 22 × 32⅛" · Amon Carter Museum, Forth Worth, Texas*

"REMINGTON," WROTE THE artist's friend and collaborator Owen Wister, "with his piercing and yet imaginative eye has taken the likeness of the modern American soldier and stamped it upon our minds with a blow as clean-cut as is the impression of the American Eagle upon our coins in the Mint."

Many of the paintings show this Americanness at a moment of crisis; others point it up with roistering humor. But in this unhurried gathering at the morning ritual of bacon and coffee, multiplied by others in the background, Remington has enabled us to enjoy most fully the truth of Wister's compliment. These are men who for a few momsnts of relaxed and even luxurious anticipation are quite at ease with each other and with themselves. However different this breakfast from those at home, it is still a link with the everyday living that war has either interrupted or permanently replaced.

The scraps of conversation here would be no more brilliant than the cuisine. But along with the meager rations and a willing horse, the good nature of them would help carry a man through the length of a dusty, unpredictable day. And the row of waiting mounts reaching away under this endless sky confirms visually, if not logically, how long the day will be.

The Scout: Friends or Enemies?

(c. 1890) *Oil on canvas · 27 × 40" · Clark Art Institute, Williamstown, Massachusetts*

R EMINGTON'S DESIRE TO BE known as artist as well as illustrator—on a more
or less equal footing—was encouraged after his first magazine appearances by his acceptance in 1887 into the galleries of the National Academy of Design and the American Water Color Society. And long before his style showed the influence of impressionism, and he began using color to heighten the mystery or excitement of a nighttime scene, individual works were proving the strength of his feeling for color emphasis. Even his so-called "black-and-white" paintings—in which the "white" may show subtle varieties of hue—are empowered by the emphasis in their blacks.

The blues that surround this Comanche scout simplify the communication of his snowy world, and most particularly the great sky-filled spaciousness of it. Remington wisely stayed close to a single-color treatment. If he had painted the man with warmer colors, an Indian and his world would not be so closely joined. And we would not follow his intent gaze as easily and freely toward the almost moon-distant line of movement he is studying.

In a narrative fashion, Remington slightly anticipates the blue Western limitlessness of a Georgia O'Keeffe.

The Old Stage Coach of the Plains

(1901) Oil on Canvas · 40¼ × 27¼" · Amon Carter Museum, Forth Worth, Texas

REMINGTON'S ENERGETIC INSTINCTS as an artist told him that the line of some far horizon was not the only way of showing the size of the West, even though it might lead the eye to mountains. A nearby up-and-down weaving like this one could work as well—especially when used imaginatively and under moonlight.

Up to and during the 1850s, before the railroads moved in, the stagecoach was the only public transportation west of St. Louis. In fact, until the joining up of the transcontinental telegraph in 1861, it was the only regular means of communicating.

The most traveled line after 1858 was the Butterfield Overland Mail, which circled south by San Antonio and El Paso at about 125 miles a day, to swing north through Yuma and Los Angeles to San Francisco. One of its Concord-built coaches is here rounding the top of a precarious-looking hill, a yellow-eyed creature staring ahead for a moment before it swoops and rattles downward. Remington painted it to illustrate an article on the Old West by Emerson Hough in the *Century Magazine.*

The loneliness of the coach is superbly dramatized against the night sky by those gleaming windows; and the rhythm of the horses' moon-cast shadows seems to offer the eye steps to climb and descend. One direction follows the coach's movement down and ahead. The other lifts us past those ghostly figures up and out into an immense night sky.

A Snowbound Christmas on the Overland Coach

(1904) Oil on canvas · 27 × 45" · Amon Carter Museum, Fort Worth, Texas

---

WHETHER OR NOT the Overland Mail was as high-flown as Remington makes it look under moonlight, there wasn't much that could stop it. A quick change of passengers or horses could, of course, or an attack by Indians or highwaymen. Or occasionally the weather.

This is one such occasion. The snow has piled up and drifted, the horses are shoulder-deep in it, and the road has disappeared. The driver up there is keeping as warm as he can—as restfully as he can—at his post of duty. And we have no idea what kind of Christmas is being celebrated inside. Or how long it will have to last. (The painting itself, you may notice, is in precarious shape.)

As a scene, it's another of a kind that appealed to Remington, and especially during his later years: people ringed around and isolated, either by other people or, as in this case, by nature. To be isolated in nature was perhaps part of the idea of going West—though not quite to this extent.

Ridden Down

(1905) *Oil on canvas · 30¼ × 51⅜″ · Amon Carter Museum, Fort Worth, Texas*

ONE EFFECT OF white penetration into the West was to throw Indian against Indian. Dislocated tribes, driven by new settlers into the regions of other tribes, found themselves in inevitable conflict. But they took it in stride. As Peter Hassrick explains in his monograph on Remington, "Only through combat could they attain social prestige among their own people; only with an honorable death could they expect to achieve rapport with their gods."

This Crow brave, his body made vivid for combat, has evidently been outnumbered and outrun by the prancing Sioux horsemen below. He and his pony have done their best, and the time has come for the final stand.

It is with picturesque irony and characteristic dramatic flair that Remington has shown this inwardly exalted Indian "ridden down" from such a spectacular height.

Victory Dance

(n. d.) *Oil on canvas · 26¼ × 35¼" · Gilcrease Institute, Tulsa, Oklahoma*

PLAINS INDIANS FOUND plenty of reasons for battling each other, from rivalry over hunting grounds to retaliation for horse stealing. The great importance was that the battle be bravely fought, with an abundance of individual daring and with as many coups counted as possible. If there was also victory, so much the better. In that case the warriors would put on whatever finery they had and return to their village whooping and singing and dancing out their triumph.

These six celebrants in the vanguard are circling their village in the kind of radiating onrush that in Remington's hands makes them seem capable of taking over the whole countryside. The troopers do something like it in *The Cavalry Charge,* and so do the exhilarated cowboys in the sculpture *Coming Through the Rye.*

The Indians, however, are not only full of noise, they're also full of news—how they won, and what each of them did. The coup stick being brandished at the center tells of one fighter's deeds. But there'll be much more than that acted out for the proud villagers before another night passes.

Through the Smoke Sprang the Daring Young Soldier

(1897) *Oil on canvas* · *27¼ × 40⅛″* · *Amon Carter Museum, Fort Worth, Texas*

REMINGTON PROBABLY DIDN'T intend the irony of this title, although his handling of the subject makes that irony all but inescapable. The oil was one of four done for *Harper's* in 1897 to illustrate the dismal saga of persecution that began with the 1876 defeat of the Northern Cheyenne under Dull Knife by a force of 1100 troopers. During the next two years the Indian survivors were intermittently harassed and herded southward toward the reservation. Finally, on a snowy January day in 1879, the small remaining band of Cheyenne men, women, and children, held captive at Fort Robinson and deprived of their rations in punishment for one who had escaped, broke from the barracks with five rifles and eleven pistols, and started north. Some ten thousand United States troops became involved in the search. About half the Indians were eventually killed, and most of the rest were recaptured.

Remington puts us behind some of the pursuing soldiers, after they finally tracked down the main group of "rebels" at a place called Warbonnet Creek. The Indians' tiny armament is making a tough fight of it. A Virginian sergeant, Carter P. Johnson, is showing great personal bravery as he springs up. But this would not seem, in the longer view, an action to inspire daring young soldiers.

Battle of Warbonnet Creek

(1897) *Oil on canvas · 26½ × 39" · Gilcrease Institute, Tulsa, Oklahoma*

A SHORT WHILE AFTER the troops' heavy fire down into Warbonnet Creek, the few remaining Cheyenne warriors have come up fighting out of the gully, led by Little Finger Nail. This apparent sequel to *Through the Smoke . . .* shows the desolate aftermath of the battle. In their very objectivity these paintings seem to be saying more than Remington himself yet comprehended concerning war as an instrument of policy.

Mari Sandoz, detailing the saga in her book, *Cheyenne Autumn,* emphasizes the Indian perspective as the troops fired into their hiding place: "The women reloaded as they could, crimping the bloated cartridges to the bullets with their teeth as long as the lead lasted. No one spoke under the thunder of the guns, the sing of the bullets, although now and then a woman or a child sobbed a little, a spasmodic sucking in of air, no more.

"'If we die in battle, our names will be remembered . . .' Little Finger Nail had said in the council down in the south country, six long moons ago. 'They will tell the story and say, "This is the place."'

"So this was the place. To this hole on a little dry creek they had come all that long and sorrowful trail."

A Reconnaissance

(1902) *Oil on canvas · 27¼ × 40⅛" · Amon Carter Museum, Fort Worth, Texas*

IN ONE OF HIS EARLY experiments in moonlit painting, Remington takes us quietly through the snow, and has us wait, huddled against the cold wind with a mounted soldier and three horses, while two others from the party peer over the crest of the ridge. The search is for Indians, who live so close to this land that they seem to disappear into it, summer or winter. But the officer ahead is determined to find some trace of life, to give his cavalry something to attack. The scout with him knows how and where to look.

The deep wintriness of Remington's scene supports the thought—whether intentionally or not—that any Indian who could find a place to rest and warm himself in these woods deserves the privacy of it. But that's not the way the West, as we say, was won.

Pony Tracks in the Buffalo Trails

(1904) *Oil on canvas · 30¼ × 51¼" · Amon Carter Museum, Fort Worth, Texas*

PURSUING INDIANS WAS difficult in any part of a country long familiar to them and strange to the invading American soldier. The mountains were full of hiding places. Out in the plains, provided the Indian kept his distance, the difficulty was one of singling out the direction of his and his ponies' movement from among the criss-crossed trails of earth-pounding buffalo.

Here a column of soldiers is having to move slowly while their own Indian scouts study the dusty ground for any traces that will point them the right way: hoof-marks, if possible; a scrap of material; or a bit of horse dung.

The sun is baking down, and Remington's generalized landscape, with just the suggestion of a butte or two in the distance, seems convincing among all the hot dust and shimmer.

The Smoke Signal

(1905) Oil on canvas · 30½ × 48¼" · Amon Carter Museum, Fort Worth, Texas

THE GREAT MOBILITY of Plains Indian life called for versatility of communications, from a signaling blanket across a mile or two to the puffs of smoke that could carry on a clear day from range to range of mountains. The smoke signal could be quick, too, even when relayed: Pawnee Indians far distant from Little Bighorn told their agent about Custer's disaster there ten days before he got the news by telegraph.

Most often signals had to do with hunting or with war. One puff, for instance, would be translated, "An enemy is near." Two single puffs, meaning "We are camping here," had to be answered carefully, since they might be luring the unwary into an enemy ambush.

Remington, at a time when he was exploring the impressionistic breaking up of color, decided to give this scene a day of unbroken stillness and clarity, and technique to match it. His three Indians and their horses, as the puffs rise from the burning grass or buffalo chips, benefit from the same clarity, and we feel in their intent watching something of the distance reached by their message. We can also enjoy incidental detail, as in the richly caparisoned saddle to the right.

The signaling part of this oil was reproduced in 1961 on a stamp celebrating the centennial of Remington's birth—the first time that the United States Post Office Department reproduced a work of art in full color.

The Stampede

(1908) *Oil on canvas · 27 × 40" · Gilcrease Institute, Tulsa, Oklahoma*

FOR A COWBOY trail-driving longhorns on the open plains, the possibility of a stampede was ever present. Many of the cowboy songs we know were designed as lullabies for the dangerous stillness of night:

O say, little dogies, when will you lie down,
And give up this shifting and roving around? . . .

But one yelping coyote, one crack of a twig, one sneeze—or one bolt of lightning—and starting with a few leaders, the herd would be on its way and soon crashing up its own thunderstorm, and the cowboys with it, working to control it.

About this richly green, weather-soaked painting, and his struggles to portray his own mental image, Remington had this to say to its purchaser: "I think the animal man was never called on to do a more desperate deed than running in the night with longhorns taking the country as it came, and with the cattle . . . all as mad as the thunder and lightning above him, while the cut banks and dog holes wait below. Nature is merciless."

Part of his success here is in the tense and convincing speed with which his mounted cowboy "takes the country." Remington, along with such other artists as Degas and Meissonier, had been able to study the action-stopping photography of men and horses by Eadweard Muybridge in the early 1880s. The swift deed is not only desperate, but convincing.

Coming and Going of the Pony Express

(1900) *Oil on canvas · 26 × 39" · Gilcrease Institute, Tulsa, Oklahoma*

JUST PRIOR TO THE Civil War the Butterfield Overland Mail, subsidized under a government contract, was the established stage route between Missouri and California. To publicize a more direct route, the competing company of Russell, Majors, and Waddell was persuaded to set up a Pony Express mail service, promising 10-day delivery at five dollars an ounce. Most of the riding was done between the furthest points of the new telegraph lines in Nebraska and Nevada. A young Buffalo Bill Cody was one of its riders, and a record of 7 days and 17 hours was set carrying Lincoln's First Inaugural.

The Overland Company soon took over the route, and subcontracted the service. The end came, after 18 months of life, with the joining up of the transcontinental telegraph.

About 190 way stations were set up, and Remington shows one of them just after the rider has changed horses. The artist has made the most of the contrast between the weary, dusty "coming" and the "going": the surge of fresh energy seems amplified by the looks and attitudes of the other men.

Cavalryman of the Line, Mexico 1889

(1889) *Oil on canvas · 24⅛ × 20⅛" · Amon Carter Museum, Fort Worth, Texas*

S OLDIERING OF ANY KIND held a fascination for Remington, and until his close look at the fighting in Cuba his feeling about war was that it was the "greatest thing which men are called on to do." So when *Harper's* asked him in 1889 to gather illustrative material in Mexico for Thomas A. Janvier's "The Aztec Treasure House," the artist took a good look at the Mexican military as well. Whether he painted this proud specimen on the spot or worked him up later from sketches and photographs, he has communicated his delight in the fine, tough, disciplined mettle of a soldier and of his mount.

Other artists—and Remington himself, in different circumstances— might have had the man *doing* something, or at least looking around, loosening up a little. But for Remington at this moment the precise formality of man and horse was the essential story, brightened by the panache of his white hat and red-bordered equipage, and eased a little by those arches in the background, opening through the stable area.

Drum Corps, Mexican Army, 1889

(c.1889) *Oil on wood · 18 ⅛ × 28 ⅛" · Amon Carter Museum, Fort Worth, Texas*

MUCH OF THE TIME on that 1889 trip for *Harper's* was spent in Mexico City, and on one sunny, dusty midday it was very well spent indeed. Through the empty streets (was it siesta time?), reverberating against the flaked stucco walls, a Mexican army corps was marching to a fusillade of drumbeats and a blare of bugles, and Remington gave it his best attention.

Though he writes of the infantry marching "loosely, with a lack of precision," that's not the way he paints their music. The men are erect, and in step; if the sandals shuffle a bit in the dust, they give every appearance of doing so in exact time.

Supporting the literal communication of it all is the slightly varied reiteration of abstract elements. Our intellectual knowledge that drums are beating is translated into the sounds themselves by Remington's strongly rhythmic sequence of shapes and movements in the drums and the arms, not to mention the fine-lined overtones around the drums and in the window-grill to the left. And to see that red-orange, high-fidelity fanfare cutting through the dust behind the drummers is surely to put in a complete sound track.

With the Eye of the Mind

(1908) *Oil on canvas · 27 × 40" · Gilcrease Institute, Tulsa, Oklahoma*

THOUGH SEEING INDIANS as inferior and often as the enemy, Remington was fascinated by their "peculiar method of thought," claiming at the same time "that no white man can ever penetrate the mystery of their mind or explain the reason of their acts."

Part of the mystery had to do with the Indian's close and deep identification with nature—an instance of which appears in this romantically conceived oil. Bathed in the last rays of a mountain sunset, with their horses already standing deep in the shadow of night, three Indians have been stopped by a vague shape in the clouds. It seems to the eye of their mind another horseman, and they read it as an omen. Though the men are placed in a tight group to the right, the leftward pull of their attention, and ours, easily balances the composition. Remington has wisely left the shape vague, so that we, too, must work at it.

Incidentally, we speak of a sunset here; but mightn't it just as credibly be a sunrise? Probably so—except that mystery is deepened by the coming rather than the going of darkness. Yet the omen could follow these Indians as meaningfully into the day as the night.

His First Lesson

(1903) *Oil on canvas · 27¼ × 40" · Amon Carter Museum, Fort Worth, Texas*

WE'RE SO ACCUSTOMED to seeing horses with saddles that it's possible to forget that the animal wasn't born to expect one. It must learn to do so. Even without the weight of a rider, the first feel of a saddle and the first tightening of a cinch belt is unexpected and frightening.

Remington chose just that moment as the subject of this painting—which also happened to be a first for him: *Collier's* accepted it for publication in color and soon contracted to pay him $1,000 each for twelve such paintings a year.

As at any such moment, the situation is precarious. Even though the young pony's right hind leg is held off the ground, the two cowboys have to be ready to move quickly as they keep control. The one on the right, acting like a man handling some kind of explosive, is stepping back and leaning forward at the same time.

Shadows reaching over from the corral gate help to steady this insecure group, to strengthen assurance that the situation will be contained and that this first lesson, at least, will be learned.

The Discovery

(n. d.) *Oil on canvas* · *27½ × 40¼"* · *Gilcrease Institute, Tulsa, Oklahoma*

INDIANS, WHILE WITHOUT a written language, had many levels of nonspoken language, and read them well. For longer distances there were signals using smoke, reflected sunlight, or the waving of robes. For close contact there was the silent sign language of the hands and arms, covering a wider range of terms and objects. And for some still simpler messages, where the giver of the message might be better off at a distance, the sign itself could be quite simple and isolated.

These two Indian scouts, followed by their pack horses, have been stopped suddenly by such a sign. They are apparently approaching a village or a camp, and in mid-trail, between two stumps, a skull is warning them not to penetrate further. They seem impressed.

Remington has added to the literal elements of the picture with his own nonspoken language. The Indians see the skull. But the strongest signals for a viewer of the painting are those two leaning stumps, and the long dead branch that snakes up from the foreground; they speak to us for the skull, and they, too, say, "Turn around, go back."

The Night Rider

(n. d.) Oil on canvas · 18 × 12" · Gilcrease Institute, Tulsa, Oklahoma

---

THE LONG, starlit silence of an Indian night, pervaded by mystery, appealed greatly to Remington during his later color-infused years of painting. This was also, of course, the ideal time for horse stealing, and at any moment the silence here could be sliced into by the swift surprise of a tribal raid.

If this rider-watchman is alert, he may hear the raiders in time to wake his own tribesmen. Whether or not the enemy can be stopped, they can be pursued and perhaps overtaken. Then there will be a battle to decide which warriors will return triumphantly to their own camp.

And Remington will have a very different scene to paint.

Missing

(1899) *Oil on canvas* · *29½ × 50"* · *Gilcrease Institute, Tulsa, Oklahoma*

HERE'S ANOTHER TITLE that implies rather than directly states, which looks, so to speak, around the corner. In this case it refers to a vantage point somewhat removed in time and in place.

The trooper being escorted by the party of Indians, with such remarkable dignity all round, will no doubt be listed in due course and somewhere else as missing. Perhaps he already is. That would be the final formality ending a chain of events, which at this moment is not quite ended. The man has been captured in battle, and he knows perfectly well that keeping prisoners is not a custom of Indian warfare. The kindest sentence he can expect is to be shot.

And however proud the bearing of Remington's Indians, the focus of his admiration—and ours—is all the more centered on this imperturbable victim of war. Stripped of his hat and his badges of rank, deprived of his horse, he is still no sheep on the way to slaughter. Without really maligning the man's captors, Remington still manages to describe him as innately superior, honoring the rightness of his cause to the end, somehow a few inches taller on his two feet than all those inscrutable warriors on horseback.

The Cowboy

(1902) *Oil on canvas · 40¼ × 27⅜″ · Amon Carter Museum, Fort Worth, Texas*

THE COWBOY IS A STUBBORN breed. One half of Remington was mourning its passage into history, the other celebrating its indestructibility. There are cowboys today who behave very convincingly as though the range were still open. The unfenceable outdoors lives in their independence, their gusty humor, their own code of responsibility.

Remington celebrated this one as part of a pictorial essay on "Western Types," run by *Scribner's Magazine* in October, 1902. The original caption—probably his own—described the cowboy as "no longer strange . . . becoming conventional, [and] merely trying to get mountain-bred ponies [down the slope at the right] to go where he wants them to go." His need to be "fast and insistent . . . represents a type of riding and pony 'footing' easier to delineate than to perform."

It's probable that most cowboys, even with this up-in-the-air "footing," would still rather perform it.

The Fall of the Cowboy

(1895) *Oil on canvas · 25 × 35⅛" · Amon Carter Museum, Fort Worth, Texas*

REMINGTON FIRST MET Owen Wister—the Western writer who also came from established Eastern stock—in 1893; and just two years later an important set of canvases was painted to illustrate Wister's article, "The Evolution of the Cow-Puncher," for *Harper's Monthly.* This somber scene is the last of the five.

"Three things swept [the puncher] away," laments Wister in his next-to-last paragraph, "the exhaustion of the virgin pastures, the coming of the wire fence, and Mr. Armour of Chicago, who set the price to suit himself . . ." Behind all these, of course, stretched the railroad, which had carried the beef to Chicago and beyond in the first place and had hurried in thousands of homesteaders and fence-builders on the longer and longer return trips.

These two cowboys—and their horses—seem heavily aware of history as one man closes the gate in a long, long wire fence, with dark lines slicing the land horizontally and vertically. Closing? There's probably no reason why he shouldn't be opening it. But everything in Remington's spacious, still, elegiac canvas suggests a closing, an end. If there are to be new beginnings, they'll have to be dealt with somewhere else, in a different mood.

The Long-Horn Cattle Sign

(1908) *Oil on canvas* · *27⅛ × 40⅛″* · *Amon Carter Museum, Fort Worth, Texas*

REMINGTON HAD ONCE pooh-poohed impressionism: "I've got two maiden aunts upstate who can knit better paintings than these." Yet in his growing desire to be more than an illustrator he was sooner or later bound to consider plein-air technique. For one thing, it would allow his usually minimal backgrounds to be more closely integrated with the painting as a whole, in their breaking up of color in response to light. Just as in the broad color areas of his nocturnal scenes, the paintings would then take on more overall interest *as* painting.

In a few late oils he drops the human subject altogether. But certainly not here. A trail driver is crossing part of a reservation with a big herd behind him, and communicates with a passing Indian in the language they both understand. His raised arm says "long-horn cattle," and the Indian's clenched fist over his heart completes his agreement for them to pass through. It may be that a few will be left to pay for the intrusion.

The sunset glow that vibrates through the colors is another result of Remington's changed mind about impressionism. But he doesn't let his "knitting" soften the rough reality of these two men.

The Bell Mare

(1903) *Oil on canvas · 34¾ × 26¾" · Gilcrease Institute, Tulsa, Oklahoma*

LONG BEFORE THERE WERE steam trains through the wilderness, there were mule trains, ready to negotiate the meandering and mountainous trails with their tough constitutions and sure feet. But like a steam train they needed something to pull them—not an engine but a bell mare. They wouldn't follow one of their own, or any other creature, up and down and around these unpredictable steeps.

But for some reason they would follow a mare anywhere—and would even insist on it. The bell round her neck helped them to know where she was; and the white coat could be a beacon in the night.

"Who can understand a mule?" wrote Remington in "Policing the Yellowstone" for *Harper's Weekly*, ". . . the old bell-mare takes across a nasty chasm or a dirty slough-hole, and as the tinkle of the little cow-bell is losing itself in the timber beyond, one after another they put their ears forward and follow on."

The Cavalry Charge

(1907) *Oil on canvas · 30⅛ × 51⅛" · Metropolitan Museum, New York City*

WE USUALLY ASSOCIATE impressionism with the peace of a Monet poppy field or a Renoir boating scene. But Remington saw in its treatment of surfaces the tremendous source of energy that exists, and he often used it to unleash that energy. He never committed himself to the full color theory of this style (and neither did Monet and Renoir in every painting); but he explored it far enough to invest this oil, for instance, with a charge beyond that of the literal subject.

The men are coming on at full tilt, revolvers at the ready. We don't see the enemy (Remington seldom shows a battle *joined*), but they can't be far away. And the encounter is already felt because in his individual way each man and each horse here is already feeling it, and because the rough, flecked texture rising from the grassy shadows into the tumult of forms above implies already the riddling of bullets. (It also makes it possible, as Remington wrote of this painting in his diary, "to paint running horses so you could feel the details instead of seeing them.")

Each man and each horse: the artist was impressed with the thorough training of the riders and their mounts that equipped them with the speed, stability, and maneuverability they needed at crucial moments like this. However, as he outlines those erect forms against the sky, he gives any approaching Indian a fine row of moving targets.

The Grass Fire

(1908) Oil on canvas · 27⅛ × 40⅛" · Amon Carter Museum, Fort Worth, Texas

THE STRONG FOCUS OF Remington's interest was almost always on the human participants in his scene; their natural surroundings might be picturesque, but still of distinctly secondary importance. His discovery of the night during his last years of painting was closely in keeping with this interest, since it enabled him with full realism to intensify the foreground drama while at least partially closing out the background.

Here the isolation of the scene is complete. Remington's only light source is the fire—it is also his dramatic focus. It gives the kind of abrupt, stagey presence to his characters (including the pony looking back at *us*) that footlights might give in the theater; and the backdrop is the impenetrable blackness of night.

Indians set fires like this as a strategy in prairie fighting. When the wind was strong and their enemy to leeward, they could pursue him under cover of the smoke, perhaps trap and even smother him. It was part of their total use of land.

The Grass Fire was one of a group of paintings done for *Collier's* in 1908, and when shown at Knoedler's inspired great critical enthusiasm for its dramatic and coloristic inventiveness.

The Outlier

(1909) *Oil on canvas · 40 × 27" · Brooklyn Museum, Brooklyn, New York*

IN THE LATTER YEARS of his life Remington continued to visit the West, but no longer to record the behavior of its people. He had already seen, as he wrote in 1905, "the living, breathing end of three American centuries of smoke and dust and sweat, and I now see quite another thing where it all took place, but it does not appeal to me."

What did still appeal to him, however, was the landscape, and he showed a few unpopulated bits of it in his 1909 show at Knoedler's. It must have pleased him greatly that the critic Gustav Kobbé admired his full and "extremely interesting" progression "from an illustrator into a painter."

But in his memory and in his big Connecticut studio he still had the people and the props to put into his paintings, and he still had the illustrator's urge to use them. This Indian is evidently posted as sentinel at a high and lonely place near his camp, and in company with the full moon he provides an evocative subject.

Lift him away, however (and in his crisper representation he *does* seem removable), and the warm bristling of the sagebrush texture could still be the basis of a fine landscape.

Or leave him there, by all means. He's eminently at home in Remington's painted world; and we might miss him.

The Bronco Buster

(1909) *Bronze · Roman Bronze Works · Height 32½" · Amon Carter Museum, Fort Worth, Texas*

THOUGH REMINGTON'S WORK in sculpture would later take in soldiers, Indians, polo players, and even prehistoric man, it was his feeling for the cowboy that most particularly invited it. And that, naturally, means the cowboy on horseback. The battle of wills between man and horse figures an interplay of mass and energy that not only epitomizes the outward excitement of the West but also figures the individual's struggle with himself.

One of Remington's friends and neighbors in New Rochelle was the sculptor Frederic W. Ruckstull. Already an admirer of the French animalier Antoine Barye, Remington watched with great interest as Ruckstull worked on a monumental equestrian statue during the spring of 1895. Ruckstull, in turn, encouraged Remington, and even set him up with the tools and some clay. By October, after a hard summer's work, the new sculptor had finished his *Buster*, which he then took to be sand-cast at the Henry-Bonnard foundry.

It went so well with the public and the critics that in 1909 he decided to give the subject a new, bigger, and still more energetic lease on life. The figure seems extra tall in the way the rider's body hangs there, his arms like wings and his legs stabbing down right over the horse's legs—with a line of rope to quicken and unite the movement.

"It will make your eyes hang out on your shirt," Remington warned Riccardo Bertelli at the Roman Bronze Works, where this work was cast.

And more than ever he felt, as he wrote Owen Wister the first time round, that "I've got a receipt for being *Great* . . . I'm doing a cowboy on a bucking broncho and I'm going to rattle down through all the ages . . ."

The Wounded Bunkie

(1896) Bronze · Henry-Bonnard Foundry · Height 20¼" · Amon Carter Museum, Fort Worth, Texas

---

THOUGH REMINGTON OFTEN confined his subjects to one cowboy, one Indian, or one soldier, the give-and-take between two or more people appealed to his energetic sense of drama—and on a secondary level he felt the same way about horses. This second of his sculptures is a kind of dramatic quartet, a complex yet skillfully unified study in living response and rhythmic movement.

Two United States cavalrymen are in action against the Indians, and the title implies that they are close friends. One has just been shot, and the other, looking in the direction of the attack, reaches over in support. At the same instant there seems to be quick rapport between the two horses.

As a sculptor Remington has challenged himself to tell the story of a fleeting incident through these complex masses without losing the swift lightness of their movement and yet containing it at the same time. He meets the challenge on both counts. The eight horse's legs carry the movement from one end to the other, while the weight rests lightly on just two of them. The effect is something like one horse at different stages of its gait.

And though the forward impulsion is strong, the leaning and turning back of the two men helps to contain it, balance it, and in a telling way unify it within this dynamically organized sculptural space.

The Cheyenne

(1901) Bronze · Roman Bronze Works · Height 21½" · Amon Carter Museum, Fort Worth, Texas

---

T HOUGH WE THINK OF the Indian as most typically a mounted fighter, he was not always so. After the sixteenth-century arrival of the Spanish *con-quistadores* under Coronado, bringing both war and the horse onto the Great Plains, the Indians there were transformed, as Russell McKee explains in *The Last West,* "from part-time farmers and rabbit eaters into colorful nomadic hunters of big game. They were men who ran at the sight of the first Spanish warriors, while with horses they became the toughest light cavalry the world had ever seen."

Remington's specimen in this 1901 bronze, modeled while he was on crutches after a fall from his own horse, shows the full change. He's a tough Indian careening ahead on a tough horse. The sculptor, never at a loss for lifting his animals in the air, manages it this time by turning a clump of sagebrush—and even a bit of the air itself—into bronze.

But he hopes this dauntless Indian can stay up there. "He had a very teetery seat," he writes Owen Wister in a joking mood, "and I am nervous about even mud [his slang for clay] riders."

The Outlaw

(1906) *Bronze · Roman Bronze Works · Height 22 ¾" · Amon Carter Museum, Fort Worth, Texas*

A COWBOY, NO DOUBT oversimplifying the formidable logistics of breaking broncs, will counsel a greenhorn to "keep a leg on each side, and your mind in the middle." Certainly there's a world more to learn—but that advice might be fairly close to the center.

Remington's mind is very much in the middle, as he lifts this bronze bronco up on his gathered-together forelegs and holds him there. It's another superb study in stability—so much so, in fact, that those two hind legs give a slight feeling of being hung in their proper place rather than being thrust up by their own kicking. The cowboy's face, too, seems surprisingly restful for this restless artist. He could be a commuter adjusting his seat on the train.

But let your eye drop from there, swing down the long curve to the horse's head, and then bounce up again to the lurching at saddle level—raising doubts as to how long the rider may be staying there—and you're into a shuddering experience that begins to take over the whole interpretation. The hind legs now become jabbing reiterations of those pile-driving forelegs.

Remington seems almost more concerned in this work with law than with outlaw. Yet the deceptively quiet up-and-down has a twisting in its spirals and a shaking in its diagonals that at least test the balance.

The Mountain Man

(1903) Bronze · Roman Bronze Works · Height 28 ⅞" · Amon Carter Museum, Fort Worth, Texas

THIS MUST COMBINE one of the steepest inclines and surest-footed beasts of burden in sculptural captivity—and quite a burden it is. The man himself is an Iroquois fur trapper of the 1830s or 40s, wearing a heavily ornamented Hudson's Bay "uniform," and he carries a half-stock flintlock and a set of beaver traps, while a piece of tanned buffalo hide eases a little the hardness of his wood-framed Indian saddle.

Remington helps us visually to feel the pony's sure grip by leaning the trapper back into an actually upright position, and then by letting the line of his upper leg follow right through into the line of the pony's right foreleg. That encourages the idea that there are not just four but six legs clinging to the mountainside—which from some vantage points could almost be believed.

This piece and *Coming Through the Rye,* purchased together by the Corcoran Gallery of Art in Washington, D.C., in 1904, were Remington's first works to be procured by a museum.

The Old Dragoons of 1850

(1905) Bronze · Roman Bronze Works · Height 25 ⅜" · Amon Carter Museum, Fort Worth, Texas

---

THE FIRST WAGON trains moving westward in the early 1840s were only lightly armed, and some were lost to Indians who resented the intrusion. Later the trains were enlarged and armed with long-range rifles, and threats to their safety were responded to by well-equipped government troops.

In 1905 Remington showed such an encounter in what is probably his most complex bronze. Four men and five horses are involved in hand-to-hand fighting, with a great variety of movement and yet with an arching of lines overhead that helps to unify and contain it.

While as a painter the artist could deal more simply with scenes such as this, and could surround them with a sky and landscape, the viewer who moves around this sculpture realizes more of the tangible presence of the action, the wholeness of each part, and the sense of forms that turn and move as the perspective changes.

The Scalp

(1898) *Bronze · Henry-Bonnard Foundry · Height 25⅞" · Amon Carter Museum, Fort Worth, Texas*

THE RATHER CONVENTIONAL posture of the horse in this bronze—its foreleg pawing the air in a monumental manner inspired by Greek, Roman, or Renaissance models—reminds us how unconventional Remington's horses usually were. They were generally kicking, rearing, leaping, stumbling, or running all-out. It's no wonder that a *Harper's Weekly* critic, Charles Coffin, made a special point in regard to this work of Remington's "serious attempt to express a moment's energy by methods reposeful and dignified."

Dignity of a masculine and often latent kind had been no stranger to the artist's work. It is present in this triumphant Indian, as his raised arm brandishes an enemy's scalp. But repose has more often to be looked for in the coherence with which Remington portrays action. Here, though not characteristic of the action itself, it is abstractly shown through the right-angled stability relating the vertical and horizontal lines of his two arms.

Technically, the work represents a transition between the sand-casting practiced at the Henry-Bonnard Foundry and the lost-wax process at the Roman Bronze Works—to which the artist turned after the Henry-Bonnard Foundry was destroyed by fire. *The Scalp,* with a few changes, was cast at both places.

The Horse Thief

(1907) *Bronze · Roman Bronze Works · Height 25¾" · Gilcrease Institute, Tulsa, Oklahoma*

AMONG WHITE SETTLERS a horse thief was the worst kind of reprobate, for whom hanging was too kind a punishment. With the Indians, on the other hand, horse raids were more or less official tribal pursuits. Horses were crucial to Indian life, and success in acquiring them was proof of a man's skill and bravery, whether shown individually or as part of a raid.

Remington was very conscious of himself as a painter when first of all he supported these swift forms not just on one piece of vegetation but on some kind of a hedge. Then he backed them up with a sheet of bronze, which might have begun by being a flapping blanket but developed into what could suggest a sheltering night sky.

He brings it off through contrast with those two gleaming bodies. The man's arms quicken the forward propulsion, and his leg, repeating the shape of the horse's shoulder, unites with an animal who seems here to deserve the Indian term, "God dog."

Paleolithic Man

(n. d.) *Bronze* · *Roman Bronze Works* · *Height 15½″* · *Gilcrease Institute, Tulsa, Oklahoma*

IN LATER YEARS Remington sometimes felt confined by the Western subjects on which he had built his short career. He certainly never abandoned them; but *Paleolithic Man* is a light-hearted instance of escape, in response to a prime topic of those days: the origins of man.

Charles Darwin had opened up the country, so to speak, and the paleontologists moved in and settled, exploring the evidence in fossils. At the turn of the century Eugene Dubois, a Dutch scientist, found human bones in Java that he estimated could be up to a half million years old, and he postulated a man from them. *Pithecanthropus Erectus* was his official name, giving him credit for standing erect. "Java Man" came more easily into the general vocabulary.

What came to Remington was a wry comment on such a man, who very likely *could* stand erect, but who finds it much more comfortable to squat, while he blinks contemplatively out of his cave. We've made such a big thing of studying him. Now it's his turn.

The Buffalo Horse

(n. d.) *Bronze · Roman Bronze Works · Height 25⅞" · Gilcrease Institute, Tulsa, Oklahoma*

To COMPARE THIS bronze with Remington's painting, *Episode of a Buffalo Hunt,* is to discover the same dynamic components: the buffalo heading one way, and the Indian hunter and his horse, stacked on top, facing even more completely in the other.

Yet the sculptured story has needed to restrain those elements of movement, and the result suggests a sudden stillness between shudders, rather than two intersecting trajectories. It is more essentially a stack.

Clearly it has to be. The buffalo and the horse could be sculptured as they are in the painting. But it would be awkward, at least, to fix the Indian out in space. So he is pulled back, arched on hands and feet above the horse's neck. The slowing of the horse's movement (its forelegs now tucked under) calls for reduced speed also in the buffalo, rearing up on its hind legs. The spear in the ground provides physical support in place of the forelegs and also helps visually to unify this remarkable study of climbing forms—of which, incidentally, only this one casting was made.

The Stampede

(1910) *Bronze · Roman Bronze Works · Height 22 ⅝" · Amon Carter Museum, Fort Worth, Texas*

A STAMPEDE WAS a tempestuous affair of great size, usually involving hundreds of cattle. A painting of it, like Remington's, could and did suggest its distances, its weather. But how could the artist expect to put the terror of this subject onto a bronze base less than four feet long?

Remington was wise enough not to try—at least not in the ground-covering terms of his 1908 painting. In the sculpture—his last completed work——he actually shows about the same number of animals. But this time the four steers are gathered so close to the cowboy that he seems to be riding them as well as his horse. And while Remington cannot here take in anything like the whole scene, through the tense rhythm of legs and horns and bodies he can tell us more tangible and empathic things about the cowboy's job at the scene.

This job is most crucially to steer the herd. The point rider, in front of the torrent, will try to head off or "haze" its leaders into a circular course, so that they may come around again to meet the main body of cattle. Perhaps by that time they will have tired enough to slow down the forward rush of the others.

Remington's cowboy is an upright figure of great concentration, controlling in his posture—especially in his curving right arm—the propulsive movement. So he suggests not chaos, but the cowboy's own remarkable and necessary control.

Trooper of the Plains

(1909) Bronze · Roman Bronze Works · Height 26¼" · Amon Carter Museum, Fort Worth, Texas

SURELY ONE OF THE canons of Remington's art was that a galloping horse has no legitimate business touching the ground. Muybridge's stop-motion photographs showed, after all, that each hoof touched down only long enough to take off again. Practically all its time is spent in the air, so that's clearly the place to show it.

To do so presents no problem, of course, in painting or drawing. But the sculptor who is not prepared, like a Calder, to suspend his forms from above must attach them from below. We've seen Remington secure horses to a clump of sagebrush, to another horse, or if necessary with two legs on the ground, and the effect of speed and lightness comes off.

In this trooper, covering immense stretches of the plains during the massive post-Civil War migration, he gathered three of the hoofs so as to join up with what again must be intended as a piece of underbrush. But it is shaped enough like a tree stump for us perhaps to find it more of an impeder than an impeller of movement. Accordingly, and because of a certain stiff exactness that grows at times from Remington's great care with detail, the figure is far less mobile than the small painted rider of a year earlier from which he had adapted it.

But there are details and perspectives to enjoy here that are denied the painting. This *Trooper* is part of Remington's full report on men and horses of the Old West.

The Wicked Pony

(1898) Bronze · The Henry-Bonnard Foundry · Height 22" · Amon Carter Museum, Fort Worth, Texas

---

IN THIS RARE bronze of Remington's (for some reason only ten castings were ever made) the usual game of bronco busting has deteriorated into a kind of wrestling match. The cowboy, out of pique at having been thrown, has grabbed his horse's ear, hoping that in this way the horse, too, will lose his balance and be thrown.

But the hope, in the actual incident on which Remington based his sculpture, was ill-founded. A few seconds later, the horse turned and gave the cowboy a devastating kick. The indiscreet buster was busted.

At this earlier stage *both* the contestants are kicking, and the artist has related them with a strong, continuous movement that swings along each body, and that focuses in the circle near the ground embracing both of their heads. The work is a composition of particular potency.

The Savage

(1908) *Bronze · Roman Bronze Works · Height 10¾" · Amon Carter Museum, Fort Worth, Texas*

REMINGTON, like many of his contemporaries, had feelings about the Indians that straddled condescension and a mystical kind of respect. They were summed up in the familiar epithet, "noble savage." The savagery in this small head speaks immediately, because the mouth is twisted to partly bare the teeth, and the slight leer that results is intensified by the high cheeks and jutting jaw.

Yet the lines of the structure surrounding the mouth communicate deep strengths: the perpendicular from the peak of the hair down through the throat tendons relates as an axis to all the horizontals of the face. This relationship is confirmed by the partly abstract base, and eased by the overall flow of the hair.

If Remington had intended irony by his title, it seems likely he would have brought the nobility nearer the surface. But the makings of irony are certainly there.

The Sergeant

(1904) Bronze · Foundry unknown · Height 10⅛" · Amon Carter Museum, Fort Worth, Texas

---

A**S A SCULPTOR**, Remington did not think in physically monumental terms. None of his works in their original form reached as much as three feet in height, and this one, the smallest of all, is just under eleven inches—*with* the artist's base.

But size and monumentality in art are relative matters. A big, perfunctory monument can seem trivial; while this Rough Rider of Roosevelt's—well-installed or well-photographed—expresses range-wide dimensions of authority and character. Essential to the effect is the simple geometry of the base and hat—an elongated cube and a full circle. The scarf serves as a transitional curve, both from one form to another and between both forms and the strongly modeled yet humanly eloquent face.

An overall singleness of statement—so important to monumentality—is also realized by the slight irregularities, even in the base; the modeling everywhere makes it all part of one sculptural idea.

The Rattlesnake

(1905) *Bronze · Roman Bronze Works · Height 23 ⅞" · Amon Carter Museum, Fort Worth, Texas*

As a subject, this sculpture belongs with the *Bronco Buster* and the other works in which the horse is acting with some degree of violence. The distinction here, of course, is that the violence is prompted not by the rider but by the danger to both horse and rider. As a sculptural object, the rattler is small—almost invisible. But Remington has used it as focus for a big movement that is one of his most effectively concerted.

We find the snake quickly, following the converging gazes of man and horse—not to mention the horse's pointing hind leg. That leg may then take us up through the arch of the horse's body, where we can move with the tight, intense, and partly closed spiral running up through the horse's forelegs and neck to curve back into the man's body and swing around at the top with his right arm.

Judging by Remington's comment, quoted by Hassrick in his monograph, it was fun playing with the position of the snake: "Just see what can be done with it—isn't it wonderful. You could work on this for days . . ." Very likely he did, off and on. But what was most importantly "done with it" shows not in the rattler itself but in the twisting harmony of the whole sculptural experience.

The Norther

(1900) *Bronze · Roman Bronze Works · Height 22" · Gilcrease Institute, Tulsa, Oklahoma*

R EMINGTON'S SCULPTURED WESTERNERS face quite a spectrum of antagonists, from Indians to rattlers to stampeding cattle, and on several occasions their own mounts. But here's a bronze in which both horse and rider are up against a less colorful but no less formidable opponent: the winter weather. People didn't discuss "wind-chill factors" in those days, yet everything about this huddled pair of creatures indicates some kind of record low— perhaps during that blizzard-devastated winter of 1887–88.

Whatever attracted him to this subject, the artist found it to be an intriguing study in textures—bitterly wind-blown textures. Most of the surface is covered with hair, including the horse's mane, tail, and winter coat, as well as the rider's chaps, and the effect on each of them is that of a wind so stiff as to be a kind of wire brush.

Indian Warfare

(1908) *Oil on canvas · 29½ × 50" · Gilcrease Institute, Tulsa, Oklahoma*

SUPPORTING HIS ESTIMATE of Remington as "one of the master American illustrators," Matthew Baigell in *The Western Art of Frederic Remington* argues that "invariably he picked the right moment, and then by combining stylistic components with startling acumen, he manipulated the viewer into accepting the authenticity of the scene. It is surprising how easy it is to remember specific Remington paintings."

This is certainly one of the unforgettable ones. A fallen brave, who would never if possible be left lying on the battlefield, has been secured under the arms by a leather rope, and is being picked up by two of his comrades, without losing a beat.

Through the pulling back of this form, and the attention given it by these warriors, the scene is fixed to a degree both within the frame and within our memories. We associate the paint on their horses' bodies and their own with what we call "savagery." But Remington the illustrator shows us in this incident some impressive men under the paint.

A Dash for the Timber

(1889) *Oil on canvas · 48¼ × 84⅛" · Amon Carter Museum, Forth Worth, Texas*

REMINGTON'S FIRST BIG commission brought about an early masterpiece. The wealthy inventor E.C. Converse, in 1889, ordered a monumental picture showing the perils of frontier life, and in *A Dash for the Timber* he certainly got it. Across its seven-foot breadth the artist spread an Arizona scene of huge energy and imminent disaster. Galloping toward us in head-long retreat are seven cowboys, nearing the scraggly fringe of a stand of trees. Close behind, and just beginning to spill onto the canvas, is a horde of Apaches in full attack. Three cowboys are firing back, and another has just been hit. Not only is "the drawing . . . true and strong," as reported in the *New York Herald,* but the men seem bound together rhythmically even as they radiate out to roar past us on both sides. A big canvas feels still bigger.

Coming Through the Rye

(1902) *Bronze · Roman Bronze Works · Height 30⅞" · Amon Carter Museum, Fort Worth, Texas*

THIS QUARTET OF Saturday-night hell-raisers was widely enjoyed during Remington's lifetime under various titles. It was *Off the Trail* when visitors saw it in an oversized version at the St. Louis World's Fair in 1904, and *Shooting Up the Town* a year later at the Lewis and Clark Exposition in Portland, Oregon. But all of its titles, including the more sophisticated one that has stuck, point to the same fact: The cowboy's work was demanding, dusty, and often lonely (there are limits, after all, to the companionability of the long-horn steer), and when he and his friends hit some otherwise quiet cow town their pent-up talents for celebration were quite noticeable.

The multiplicity of figures here, suggesting in their rise and fall and in the raised arms the working of a carousel, enabled Remington to do something that must have plased him particularly. That was to get one horse and rider completely off the ground or any appurtenance thereof, and all the others well on their way.